ANGLO-SAXONS

Written by Anita Ganeri

W
FRANKLIN WATTS

Franklin Watts
Published in paperback in Great Britain in 2019
by The Watts Publishing Group
Copyright © The Watts Publishing Group, 2017
All rights reserved.

Editor: Sarah Silver
Designer: Luke Kelly
Picture researcher: Diana Morris

ISBN 978 1 4451 5209 7

Printed in China

Franklin Watts
An imprint of
Hachette Children's Group
Part of The Watts Publishing Group
Carmelite House
50 Victoria Embankment
London EC4Y 0DZ

An Hachette UK Company
www.hachette.co.uk

www.franklinwatts.co.uk

Contents

Who were the Anglo-Saxons?

In 43 CE, the Romans invaded Britain and ruled for around 400 years. The last Roman soldiers left Britain in 410 CE, and new peoples began to invade. They came from Germany, Denmark and Holland, part of the Netherlands. We call them the Anglo-Saxons. They arrived in southern England first, and gradually pushed their way north.

Warriors and farmers

Some of the Anglo-Saxons were warriors, who came to fight for power. Others came peacefully, looking for fertile land to farm. Back home, the land often flooded, making it difficult to grow enough food. Whole families set off in small wooden boats, across the North Sea, bringing their weapons, tools and even farm animals with them.

People acting the part of Anglo-Saxon warriors.

4

Anglo-Saxon times

Around 400 CE	Anglo-Saxons begin to arrive in Britain
410	The Romans leave Britain for good
597	Augustine sent to convert the Anglo-Saxons to Christianity
600	Seven Anglo-Saxon kingdoms created
793	The Vikings attack Lindisfarne Priory
871	Alfred the Great becomes King of Wessex
927	Athelstan becomes King of the English
1016	The Viking Cnut (Canute) rules Britain
1042	The Anglo-Saxon king, Edward the Confessor, is crowned
1066	Battle of Hastings ends Anglo-Saxon rule

Anglo-Saxon Chronicle

In the 9th century, King Alfred ordered monks to begin writing a history book about the Anglo-Saxons. It was called the *Anglo-Saxon Chronicle*, and is one of our main sources of information about life in Anglo-Saxon times. The chronicle gives a year by year account of harvests, battles and other important events, over a period of over a thousand years. Many copies of the original were made and sent to monasteries all over England, where the monks kept them up to date.

WRITING HISTORY

Much of what we know about history comes from written accounts and records. Some of these were written at the time; others much later on. Throughout this book, you will find panels asking you to write your own versions of the history you have read. You will find the information you need in the book, but you can also look online and in other books. Use the tips provided, and don't be afraid to let your imagination run wild.

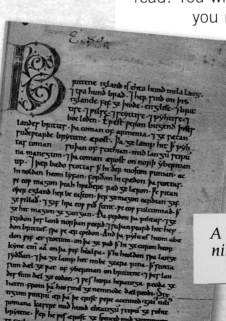

A page from one of the nine remaining Anglo-Saxon Chronicles.

Anglo-Saxon life

Most ordinary Anglo-Saxons lived in small villages, with several other families. Houses were built from wood, with thatched roofs. The thane (noble) who was head of the village, lived in a large hall in the middle of the village, and owned the fields all around. Churls (ordinary people) had smaller houses. They had to promise to fight for their thane if he needed them, in return for land to farm.

Growing up

There were no schools in Anglo-Saxon times, and most children could not read or write. Girls helped their mothers at home. They were taught housekeeping skills – how to cook, weave cloth on a loom, make clothes and brew ale. Boys helped their fathers to plough the fields, bring in the harvest, hunt, catch fish, chop wood and use weapons. In their free time, they played with homemade toys, such as rag dolls and wooden animals. They also played board games, with counters and dice.

You can visit this reconstructed Anglo-Saxon village in Suffolk.

What to wear

Ordinary Anglo-Saxons wore clothes woven from rough wool, though richer people could afford finer wool or linen. Men and boys wore tunics with leggings or trousers. They held their trousers up with leather belts, which were also useful for hanging pouches and knives from. Women and girls wore long dresses with belts. In cold weather, both men and women wore thick, woollen cloaks, fastened with metal pins or brooches.

Children wore long tunics similar to those worn by these modern-day child re-enactors.

Looms were used to weave cloth for clothes. This loom is an historical copy.

Did you know?

Both men and women wore jewellery in Anglo-Saxon times. They made necklaces and bracelets from glass and amber beads, and gemstones, such as amethysts. Wealthy people could afford beautiful gold and silver necklaces and brooches.

Helmets and shields similar to these reconstructions were made by metalworkers.

Jobs and work

In an Anglo-Saxon village, people had to work very hard to survive. Everyone – men, women and children – helped on the farm, growing crops, such as wheat, barley and rye, and keeping animals, such as cows, sheep and pigs. Some of the villagers had special craftworking skills. Woodworkers made furniture, carts and chests. Potters made pots and dishes for cooking and eating. Metalworkers made iron tools, knives and swords, as well as beautiful gold and silver jewellery for wealthy people.

Write a job advert

A job has come up in an Anglo-Saxon village for someone to make tools, swords and jewellery. Can you write a job advert for a metalworker? Have a look at some adverts in the newspaper or online to find out how to create your advert.

Everyday food

From day-to-day, most families ate simple meals of bread, oat porridge and stew made from the vegetables – onions, peas, cabbage and parsnips – that they grew. They sometimes had eggs, cheese and milk, and fish, caught in the river or sea. Food was cooked in a large metal pot, which hung down from a chain over the fire in the middle of the house. Meals were washed down with weak ale, rather than water which was too dirty to drink.

Write a feast invite

Imagine that you are the village thane, about to hold a lavish feast. You want the thane of a neighbouring village to be your guest of honour. Write an invitation to the feast. Look at some party invites for inspiration. Remember to include the time and location of the feast.

This detail from the Bayeux Tapestry (see page 27) shows an Anglo-Saxon king at a feast.

HIC

9

Language and writing

The Anglo-Saxons spoke a language called Old English. Early on, it was written down using symbols, called runes (see right). When the Anglo-Saxons became Christians (see pages 18–21), they began to use the Roman alphabet that we still use to write English today.

Runes had straight lines which made them easier to carve into wood, stone or metal.

Did you know?

Many words used in English today come from Old English, though their spellings and pronunciations have changed.

faether = father
sunu = son
dohtor = daughter
hunig = honey
aeg = egg
chese = cheese

Bede, shown here in a 12th-century manuscript, wrote his book in Latin, completing it in 731. It was translated into Old English later.

HISTORY BOOK

Anglo-Saxon monks wrote the first-known English history books. One famous book was written by a monk, called Bede (673-735), who lived in a monastery at Jarrow in north-east England. The book, *The Ecclesiastical History of the English People*, tells the history of England and of Christianity, from 55 BCE, when Roman leader, Julius Caesar, invaded.

Imagine that you are an Anglo-Saxon child whose family has left its home in Germany to settle in England. Write a diary about your new life. The first day has already been written. Using the information in this chapter, can you fill the rest of the week? You can write about getting new clothes, going to a feast, helping your parents in the fields and learning new skills.

Monday

Today, I helped Dad build our new house. We chopped some wood to make a door and collected reeds to thatch the roof. It'll be great when it's finished and we can move in. We had some bread and cheese for lunch, then I went fishing with my friends.

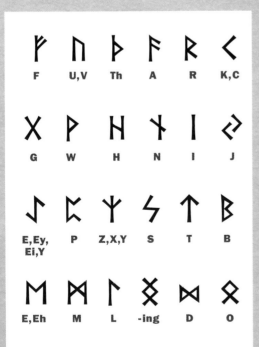

Use the runes above to add a secret message to your diary.

WRITING HINTS AND TIPS

- Write your diary in the first person, using the past tense.
- Write down events in the order they happened (chronological order).
- Remember to add your own thoughts and feelings about events.
- If your diary is secret, you can use notes and informal language.
- Don't forget to write the day and date on each entry.

Kings and kingdoms

Gradually, the different groups of Anglo-Saxon settlers grew larger, led by a war chief. A particularly strong or powerful chief became a king. Each king led a small army of loyal warriors who swore to fight to the death for him. By around 600, the most powerful kingdoms in England were Northumbria, Mercia, Wessex, and East Anglia. They were frequently at war with each other.

A person playing King Harold II in a re-enactment of the Battle of Hastings (see page 27).

There were seven main Anglo-Saxon kingdoms in England in the 7th century.

Viking threat

From the end of the 700s, the Anglo-Saxons faced another threat. Vikings from Scandinavia began to raid England. In 793, they attacked the monastery of Lindisfarne in Northumbria, burning buildings, stealing treasures and killing monks. The *Anglo-Saxon Chronicle* noted: 'This year came dreadful fore-warnings over the land … these were immense sheets of light rushing through the air, and whirlwinds, and fiery dragons flying across the firmament. These tremendous tokens were soon followed by a great famine.'

RAID WRITING

An Anglo-Saxon monk, called Simeon, wrote about the raid in his *History of the Church of Durham*: '… they reached the church of Lindisfarne, and there they miserably ravaged and pillaged everything; they trod the holy things under their feet, they dug down the altars, and plundered all the treasures of the church. Some of the brethren they slew, some they carried off with them in chains, the greater number they cast out of doors, and some they drowned in the sea.'

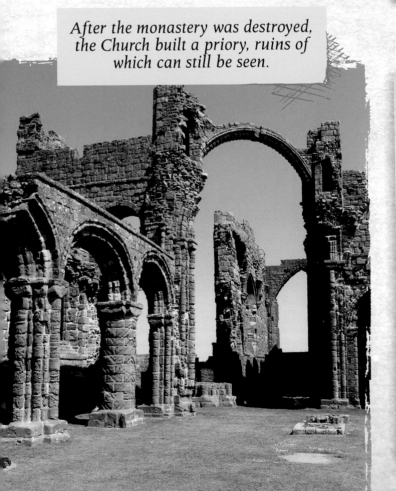

After the monastery was destroyed, the Church built a priory, ruins of which can still be seen.

Write a ransome note

Imagine that you are a young monk, captured by the Vikings. They are holding you to ransom. Write a quick note to your family, telling them what has happened, and how much money it will take to rescue you. Make it short and snappy — you don't have much time!

Famous kings

Offa (ruled 757–796)

During Offa's reign, Mercia became the most powerful kingdom in England, and Offa the most important king. He is probably best known for building a huge earth wall and ditch between Mercia and Wales, to keep the Welsh out of his land.

Aethelwulf (ruled 839–856)

Aethelwulf was King of Wessex. He and his sons fought many battles against Viking raiders from Denmark. Deeply religious, Aethelwulf made a pilgrimage to Rome in 855. Four of Aethelwulf's sons became king after him, including the youngest, who went on to become Alfred the Great (see pages 16-17).

A long part of this wall, called Offa's Dyke, can still be seen today.

A 14th-century manuscript showing Aethelwulf.

Did you know?

Offa issued new penny coins made from silver. They showed Offa's head in the style of a Roman emperor. From then on, all English coins showed the ruler's image and name.

Athelstan (ruled 924–939)

The grandson of Alfred, Athelstan became King of Mercia, then of Wessex. A brilliant soldier, he expanded his kingdom by capturing York, and then Northumbria. In 937, he defeated the Vikings at the Battle of Brunanburh.

Eadgar (ruled 959–975)

Eadgar came to the throne of Wessex when he was 16 years old. It is said that he was a very short man and very handsome. His reign was largely peaceful. The monasteries flourished and became centres of learning. He also built up a large navy to guard against Viking raids.

This 10th century manuscript shows King Athelstan presenting a book to Saint Cuthbert.

A Victorian illustration of King Eadgar.

Write a biography

Write a biography of one of the Anglo-Saxons kings. You should include their name, important dates (birth, death reign), and any special features. Add a summary of their greatest achievements, and complete your biography with a small portrait.

King Alfred (ruled 871–899)

The most famous Anglo-Saxon king was Alfred, known as Alfred the Great. As King of Wessex, he drove the Danish Vikings back in 878, then later made peace with them. The two sides agreed to divide England between them. Alfred ruled in the south and west, while the Danes ruled in the north and east (the Danelaw). Alfred made Winchester his capital. In 886, he captured London and was named King of England.

This statue of Alfred the Great was built in 1899, 1,000 years after his death.

Burning the cakes

Legend says that, one day, Alfred was forced to hide from the Vikings. He took shelter in a poor cowherd's house, on a marshy island in Somerset. Not knowing who he was, the cowherd's wife left him to watch some cakes (or bread) that she was cooking on the fire. Busy thinking about the Viking threat, Alfred accidently let the cakes burn and he was scolded by the woman when she returned.

Did you know?

Alfred was a great scholar. Another legend tells how Alfred's mother promised a book of Saxon poems to the first of her sons who could read it and learn it by heart. Alfred won the book and he was only four years old!

Writing History: News Report

Imagine that you are an Anglo-Saxon journalist sent to investigate the story of King Alfred burning the cakes. You have to write a newspaper report. Try to give both sides of the story. How did the woman feel when she found out that her guest was King Alfred? Did the king make any comment? Here's the opening paragraph to get you started.

The Daily Saxon

Sometime in 878
Somerset, England

KING IN CAKE SHOCKER!

A local woman was still in shock today after discovering the identity of the man accused of burning her best cakes.

'It still hasn't sunk in,' she said. The man, who didn't want to be named, had been sheltering in her house from the Vikings when the incident happened.

An illustration showing the story of Alfred and the cakes.

WRITING HINTS AND TIPS

- Start your report with a catchy headline to grab your reader's interest.
- The first paragraph should be exciting but not give too much away.
- Next, describe what happened, and when and where it happened.
- Add quotes from people who were there at the time.
- Look at a newspaper in print or online to get some ideas.

Beliefs and culture

Many of the Romans in Britain had been Christians but the early Anglo-Saxons were pagans. When they arrived in England, they brought their own beliefs with them. They believed in many different gods and goddesses who ruled over the world and controlled what happened in people's lives. The king of the gods was Woden (see below). Thunor was god of thunder; Tiw, god of war, and Frige, goddess of love.

This illustration of Woden was produced in the 12th century. Some of the names of the days of our week come from the Anglo-Saxon gods – for example, Wednesday comes from Woden's day.

Lucky charms

The Anglo-Saxons were very superstitious. To protect themselves from illness and evil spirits, they put lucky amulets in their homes or wore them around their necks. Some amulets were parts of plants, such as nuts or strips of bark. Others were made from animal bones, teeth, pebbles and shells.

An Anglo-Saxon amulet.

Becoming Christians

In 597, the Pope, the head of the Christian Church in Rome, sent a monk, called Augustine, to England. His task was to convert the Anglo-Saxons to Christianity. Augustine landed in Kent, in southern England, where he met King Ethelbert. The king allowed him to build a church at Canterbury, his capital, and later became a Christian himself. Over the next 100 years, most Anglo-Saxons became Christians, and many churches and monasteries were built in England.

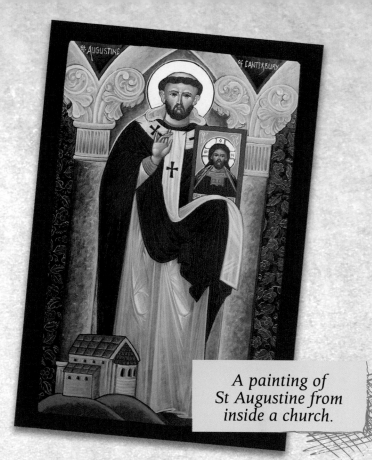

A painting of St Augustine from inside a church.

Did you know?

According to Bede (see page 10), King Ethelbert agreed to meet Augustine and to hear what the monk had to say. But he insisted that the meeting take place outdoors. He believed that Augustine had come to practice witchcraft but that this 'magic' could only work inside a building.

You can see some original Anglo-Saxon church features at Saint Peter's Church in Sunderland, which was originally built in the 7th century.

Monks and monasteries

Some Christians became monks, like Augustine. They lived in monasteries, where they dedicated their lives to God. Monasteries also became centres of learning. To record events, the monks made beautiful, illuminated manuscripts, which they copied out by hand. Often, they decorated the pages and margins with letters and designs.

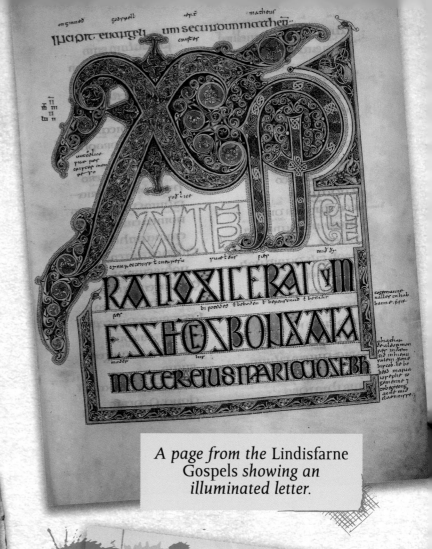

A page from the Lindisfarne Gospels *showing an illuminated letter.*

Lindisfarne Gospels

The *Lindisfarne Gospels* is a famous illuminated manuscript, written in around 700 by a monk, called Eadfrith, from Lindisfarne Priory in Northumbria. The pages are richly decorated and the book was originally bound in leather, covered in metals and jewels. During the Viking raid on Lindisfarne (see page 13), this cover was lost. The pages themselves were saved, and are on display in the British Library in London.

Create an illuminated manuscript

Try creating your own manuscript, focusing on an important day in your life. Start your manuscript with a colourful illuminated letter — this could be the initial of your name. Look at the letter in the picture above and base your design on it.

Stories and riddles

At feasts (see page 9), the Anglo-Saxons loved telling riddles. The riddle below is about a creature and its home – can you guess what it is? (Answer at bottom of page.)

My home is not quiet
but I am not loud.

We are meant to
travel together.

I am faster than he
and sometimes stronger,

But he keeps on going
for longer.

Sometimes, I rest but he
runs on.

For as long as I am alive,
I live in him.

If we part from
one another,

It is I who will die.

Write a riddle

Try writing your own Anglo-Saxon riddle. Remember to include lots of clues about what the object is. Your riddle doesn't have to rhyme but it should have a strong rhythm or beat because it is meant to be spoken out loud. Plenty of dramatic language is a must!

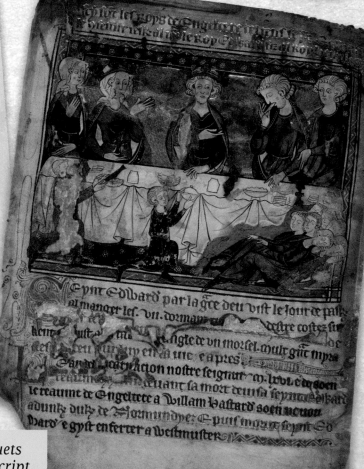

Riddles were told at feasts and banquets like the one in this 13th century manuscript, showing Edward the Confessor.

Answer: A fish in a river

Anglo-Saxon stories

At a feast, a storyteller kept guests entertained with stirring tales of brave heroes, great battles and hideous monsters. Anglo-Saxon stories took the form of long poems to be learned by heart and recited out loud. They were not written down until much later on. The Anglo-Saxons loved dramatic language and alliteration, which added to the sing-song effect, and helped the storyteller to memorise the lines.

Did you know?

The Anglo-Saxons used many interesting phrases, called kennings. A kenning described something ordinary in an extraordinary way. Can you guess what these kennings mean?

a) Whale-road b) Battle-sweat
c) Bone-house d) Sky-candle

(Answers at bottom of page)

A modern illustration of an Anglo-Saxon storyteller at a feast.

Beowulf

One of the Anglo-Saxons' favourite poems was *Beowulf*. In the story, a terrible monster, called Grendel, attacks the Danish kingdom of King Hrothgar. A young warrior from Sweden, called Beowulf, kills Grendel. Back home, Beowulf is crowned king. He rules peacefully for 50 years. Then, a fire-breathing dragon threatens the kingdom, and people beg the king for help. Brave Beowulf kills it but is fatally wounded, and dies.

An illustration showing Beowulf defeating Grendel.

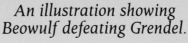

Answers: a) the sea; b) blood; c) the body; d) the sun

Writing History: Anglo-Saxon poem

Imagine that you are an Anglo-Saxon storyteller, writing a new version of *Beowulf*. Pack it with exciting language and dramatic kennings. Remember to keep reading it out loud to check that the rhythm is strong. An idea for the beginning of the poem is given on the right.

Now, let me tell you of King Hrothgar of Denmark.
Who built a huge hall on top of a hill.
By rights, it should have been happy,
Filled with feasting, fine food and song.
But, outside in the ink-stained hour,
Lurked a deadly danger too dreadful to speak –
none other than gruesome Grendel,
the devious devil from hell.

A page from the 1,000 year-old Beowulf *manuscript*.

WRITING HINTS AND TIPS

- Pack your poem with alliteration, in the Anglo-Saxon style.
- Leave pauses in the middle of lines so you can take a breath.
- To get a good rhythm, clap as you read your poem out loud.
- For kennings, take an object and write down lots of connected words.
- Read other versions of *Beowulf* in books or online.

Anglo-Saxons at war

The Anglo-Saxons were fierce warriors but mostly fought part-time. They went into battle if their king or chief ordered them to. Most were also farmers – after a battle, they went back home to look after their animals and crops. Warriors followed a strict 'warrior code'. It taught that a warrior should be brave and loyal, ready to fight to the death for his leader. This would have been an honourable way to die.

Weapons and armour

We know about Anglo-Saxon weapons and armour because some warriors were buried with them (see pages 28–29). Warriors wore iron helmets and thick, leather waistcoats or chainmail shirts.

They fought on foot, with spears, swords, battle-axes and wooden shields. In battle, warriors stood side-by-side and formed a 'shield-wall' by overlapping their shields. Then they charged at the enemy.

A re-enactment of Anglo-Saxon warriors preparing for battle.

Famous battles

The most famous battle in Anglo-Saxon times was the Battle of Hastings in 1066 (see page 27), but there were many others. The Battle of Maldon was fought in August 991 in Essex, between the Anglo-Saxons and an army of Vikings from Norway. Accounts of the battle tell how the Anglo-Saxon leader, Byrhtnoth, allowed the Vikings to cross the river for a fair fight on the shore. Sadly for him, Byrhtnoth's generosity backfired, and the Anglo-Saxons lost the battle. Byrhtnoth himself was killed.

Battle verse

One account of the Battle of Maldon is given in an Anglo-Saxon poem of the same name. It was written from the Anglo-Saxon viewpoint, shortly after the battle. Today, only 325 lines of the poem survive, and both the beginning and end are missing.

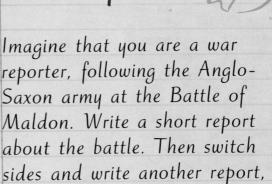

Write a war report

Imagine that you are a war reporter, following the Anglo-Saxon army at the Battle of Maldon. Write a short report about the battle. Then switch sides and write another report, this time from the Vikings' point of view.

You can see this statue of Byrhtnoth in Maldon, Essex.

Viking take-over

After King Eadgar (see page 15), the Vikings were able to win back their lands. In 1016, a Danish Viking, called Cnut, became king of England. When he died in 1035, his two sons became king in turn. But, in 1042, England had an Anglo-Saxon king again, Edward the Confessor. He got his name because he was deeply religious and often confessed his sins.

A stone statue of Edward the Confessor in Staffordshire. He ruled England for 24 years.

The Norman Conquest

When Edward died in 1066, Harold, Earl of Wessex, was declared king. Almost immediately, he found himself fighting for his throne. In September, he defeated a Viking force, led by the Norwegian, Harald Hardrada, at the Battle of Stamford Bridge in Yorkshire. Then, he hurried his army south to from an even bigger threat coming from Normandy (part of modern-day France).

Stamford Bridge, Yorkshire, today.

The Battle of Hastings

Harold has another rival to his throne – William, Duke of Normandy, the cousin of Edward the Confessor. William claimed that Edward had promised that he would be the next king of England. On 28 September, William landed on the south coast of England. Two weeks' later, he faced Harold's army at the Battle of Hastings. The battle lasted all day, with heavy losses on either side. Harold was killed and William 'the Conqueror' became king. The Anglo-Saxon period was over.

Did you know?

A popular legend says that Harold was killed by an arrow through the eye, but nobody knows for certain. While one Norman account tells that he was hacked down by four Norman knights, another says that he died from an arrow wound to his head.

Tapestry record

There are many written accounts of the Norman Conquest but the most famous record is the Bayeux Tapestry. This 70-m tapestry is embroidered on linen, using coloured wools. It was probably made in the 1070s in Canterbury. It tells the story, scene by scene, ending with the Battle of Hastings.

A scene from the Bayeux Tapestry showing the Battle of Hastings.

How do we know?

We know about the Anglo-Saxons from manuscripts and poems, but archaeologists have also found many Anglo-Saxon artefacts. Perhaps their most amazing find came in the 1930s, at Sutton Hoo in Suffolk. Here, they discovered the grave of an Anglo-Saxon king, who had been buried inside a wooden boat, underneath a huge mound of earth.

The Sutton Hoo boat.

A royal burial

As was the custom with the pagan Anglo-Saxons, the king's body was placed in a burial chamber and surrounded by the many objects that he would need in the afterlife. These included weapons, jewellery, clothes, drinking cups and even a purse full of coins – a very rich treasure trove. Archaeologists think that this may have been the grave of King Redwald of East Anglia who died in around 625 and clearly was an important man.

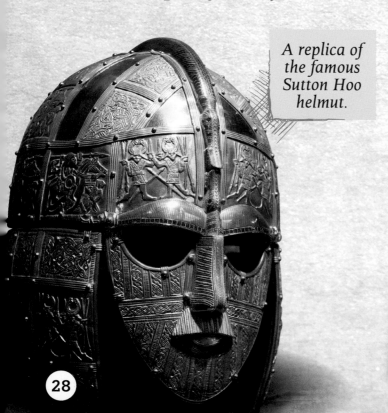

A replica of the famous Sutton Hoo helmut.

Describe an artefact

Imagine that you are an archaeologist, cataloguing the artefacts found at Sutton Hoo. Write a short description of one of the artefacts, such as the famous helmet. Remember to say where and when it was found, and what it might have been used for.

WRITING History: Eyewitness account

Imagine that you are one of King Redwald's loyal warriors, attending his burial at Sutton Hoo. You help to lay the dead king's body in the ship, and place his treasures, including his trusty sword, around him. Write an eyewitness account of the burial ceremony. The opening few lines have been written for you.

In the year 625
In the kingdom of East Anglia

I, Aelfric the warrior, son of Aelfwig, did today attend the burial of my dear lord and friend, King Redwald of East Anglia. It was a solemn day that I shall not forget. My lord fell in battle a week back. He was brave until the end.

WRITING HINTS AND TIPS

- Use your imagination to put yourself in the warrior's place.
- Descriptive language will help the reader feel as if they are there.
- Write about how the ceremony, and the king's death, made you feel.
- Use quite formal language in your account.
- Organise your account into paragraphs to make it easier to read.

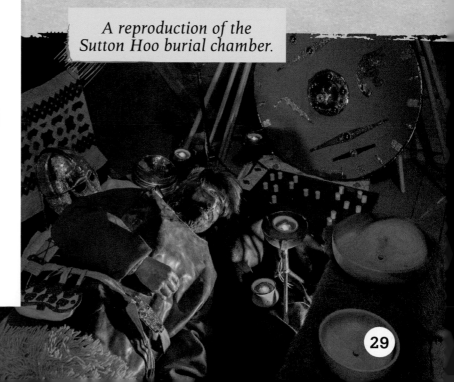

A reproduction of the Sutton Hoo burial chamber.

Glossary

afterlife The belief that a person lives on in a different world after they have died.

alliteration When words in a sentence begin with the same letter or sound.

archaeologist A person who finds and studies places and objects from the past.

artefact An object made by a person, usually referring to the past.

biography The life story of a person, written by someone else.

brethren The members of an organisation or religious group.

cataloguing Recording something, especially in a list.

Christian A person who follows the teachings of the Christian Church.

chronicle A written record of historical events.

cowherd A person who cares for grazing cattle.

Danelaw The part of England ruled by the Vikings from the 9th century until 1066.

domestic Something that is connected to the home, house or family.

fertile Land that can produce a large number of crops.

firmament Another word for the sky.

illuminated A text written by monks, that was decorated with gold and coloured paint, and small pictures.

Latin The language spoken by the ancient Romans.

monastery A building in which monks live and worship.

Normans People from Normandy (now in northern France) who invaded England in 1066, led by William the Conqueror.

Old English The earliest form of the English language, spoken by the Anglo-Saxons.

pagan A person who follows an ancient religion that worships many different gods, often linked to nature.

pilgrimage A journey made to a place that is considered special to a religion.

pillage To steal things from a place or region using violence, usually in a war.

plunder To steal valuable things from a place, often using violence.

priory A small monastery or nunnery governed by a prior or prioress.

riddle A question that describes things in a difficult or confusing way, and has a clever or funny answer.

rune A letter of the Anglo-Saxon alphabet that was designed to be cut into stone or wood.

saint A very good and holy person.

Scandinavia The area of northern Europe that includes Denmark, Sweden and Norway.

superstitious Believing in something that is based in magic and not in scientific knowledge or reason.

thane In Anglo-Saxon times, a noble who helped the king to rule.

thatched Having a roof made from straw or reeds.

Viking People from Scandinavia who began to attack England at the end of the 700s.

Further Information

Websites

www.britishmuseum.org/learning/schools_and_teachers/resources/cultures/anglo-saxons_and_vikings.aspx
Explore the British Museum's collection of Anglo-Saxon artefacts.

www.show.me.uk/tag/anglo-saxon
Information and activities relating to the Anglo-Saxon period.

www.nationaltrust.org.uk/sutton-hoo
Find out about the discovery of the Sutton Hoo ship burial, and the story behind the site.

www.bayeuxtapestry.org.uk/
See the Bayeux Tapestry online and find out more about its fascinating history.

Books

Britain in the Past: Anglo-Saxons by Moira Butterfield (Franklin Watts, 2015)
A Child's History of Britain: Life in Anglo-Saxon Britain by Anita Ganeri (Raintree, 2014)
Horrible Histories: Smashing Saxons by Terry Deary (Scholastic, 2016)

Index